Asking In

Six Empowering Questions Only You Can Answer

by
Stephanie Noble

Asking In

Six empowering questions only you can answer

Both/And Books

ISBN 978-0-9638088-1-3

stephanienoble.com

Cover photo credit: Marita King

Cover design: Adrian Emery

Quill icon: Freepik

For my husband of fifty years, Will Noble,
who always has me asking myself
"How did I get so lucky?"

Introduction

Do you ever wonder…?

Of course, you do! Wondering is an attribute of being human. Our innate curiosity and our ability to ponder complex questions has been key in our development as a species. Some of our questions are practical with answers available at our fingertips or voice command. But there are other questions only we can answer for ourselves. If we are willing to ask and willing to listen in, we can live with greater ease, joy, and clarity. But not all questions are created equal. Some are downright toxic. Others may be interesting but ultimately unanswerable, leaving us exhausted and no more enlightened.

I have found the six questions I share in this book to be especially illuminating. They shine a warm light on any situation or quandary we may be in, and they prompt answers that free us to live joyfully with a sense of meaning and purpose.

These six questions are offered in a specific order: questions #1, #2 and #3 help us to find a sense of safety in ourselves, our lives and in the world. Questions #4 and #5 help us find a sense of satisfaction. And Question #6 helps us find meaningful connection.

Safety, satisfaction, and connection. To readers and students of psychologist, neuroscientist, and New York Times bestselling author Dr. Rick Hanson, these three words together may sound familiar. He says that humans have three main concerns in this specific order: safety, fulfillment and connection. It was only after hearing Rick interviewed about his new book that I saw that this was exactly the order I was teaching these six questions. Coincidentally, as a guest teacher for Rick's meditation group, I shared this series of questions with his students over a period of weeks.

The order makes sense: if we don't feel safe, we don't care about anything else in that moment. Once we have a roof over our head, good health, food in our belly and no immediate threat of losing these things, we begin to seek meaningful satisfaction in our lives. Only after we've defined, allowed and encouraged the development of our interests can we truly connect with others in a mutually beneficial way. Safety, satisfaction and connection -- the six questions shared in this book guide us in a rich exploration through each of these.

But what do we mean by questioning? This process is not like a job interview or a criminal interrogation. Any attempt to 'grill' ourselves will cause misery. Instead, we allow our natural curiosity to blossom. That's the only way we can produce anything fruitful.

How to Use This Book

To get the most benefit out of what follows, read the chapters in order, taking as much time you need between them to explore what comes up for you. Allow yourself to go back to previous chapters as needed. Do the exercises as many times as you like; this is an ongoing process. These questions activate your own inner wisdom and tune your ability to hear that still quiet voice within that is ready and able to guide you through even the most difficult times.

Inquiry is best done after a period of quiet unplugged relaxation, either meditation or just a few minutes of silence. If you don't meditate but would like to try it, I offer guidance at the end of this book.

Keep the process alive, try things out, notice how the questions solve problems and create interesting challenges.

Be discerning in your inner investigation. Authentic answers have a quite different quality than ones that are loud, urgent and demanding to be heard. Without making an enemy of anything that arises, cultivate spacious awareness so that your wisdom is welcomed.

Throughout this book are pages for you to make notes and answer the questions for yourself. Each time you revisit the questions, your notes become more valuable. If you prefer, keep a journal, use it to take notes, do exercises, and track any shifts that happen in your life and any insights you may have. Either way, you will have a personalized aid full of customized answers, and a reminder that this process of questioning is fruitful.

Please let me know how it goes, and what you discover after asking yourself these six empowering questions.

— *Stephanie Noble*
stephanienoble.com

Are you asking yourself toxic questions?

My mind is like a bad neighborhood. I try not to go there alone.

—Anne Lamott

Inquiry is an intrinsic part of the Insight Meditation tradition. After a meditation session, we are usually more relaxed and mindful. It can be a fruitful time to do some self-inquiry. As we develop a regular meditation practice, the mind becomes more spacious, resilient, compassionate and wise, and the inquiry is rich and full of insights, both subtle and profound.

In the coming chapters we will explore six empowering life-enhancing questions. But first, let's look at the very different kinds of questions we often have rattling around in our thoughts that act more like weapons than tools. We may not even be aware of them, but they cause harm to ourselves and others.

I imagine you have at least one habitual question that can trip you up and take you down. It stops you from doing what you want to do or gets in the way of meaningful relationships. If you can identify it, congratulations!

Once we notice a question, we may need to remind ourselves not to make an enemy of it. Instead, it helps to see it as a messenger, misguided but trying to protect us. These messages are rooted in fear and prevent us from living full and meaningful lives. We can respectfully decline to take such advice.

Examples of toxic questions

'Why me?'

Things aren't going well. Maybe multiple difficulties happen around the same time. Who can blame us for wondering 'why me?' However, if this question is a persistent pattern of 'why me?' then there is a habit of looking through a narrow lens focused only on how things affect us personally, without concern for how they impact others. For example, through the family grapevine, we hear that a relative is gravely ill. A wholesome mind will register the sense of shock, worry and sadness this brings up personally. But it will also expand to focus on the people most affected: the ill person and their immediate family. Quite naturally, a wholesome mind will reach out to help or send supportive words. But with a narrow-focused lens, on hearing the news, the unwholesome mind will say, 'Why is this happening to me now? I'm under so much stress already.'

We can see how the habitual 'why me?' question is unskillful, but we can also recognize that it is a messenger: it tells us to spend more time cultivating awareness and compassion, bringing ourselves into balance.

'Who's to blame in this situation?'

In any relationship — at home, at work, in any group — things happen that weren't intended, causing problems that need to be handled. In that moment, how useful is it to point fingers and assess blame? There may be a time later when all involved look at how to avoid such problems in the future, but immediately going into blame mode is not useful.

Faultfinding may be a default pattern you inherited that is worth noticing and reconsidering. Noticing it doesn't make you wrong, it makes you wise. It's the first step to letting down your defenses and appreciating being an integral part of a relationship.

"Why am I so stupid?" "Why am I such an idiot?" "What is wrong with me?"

These are the questions that class members discovered that they say to themselves (or used to say to themselves and now realize they no longer do. Yay!) This kind of self-abuse needs to be noticed.

A classic way of considering whether this is skillful is to ask yourself if you would say that to a friend. If any friend would dump you for saying such things, then why on earth is it okay to say it to yourself?

"Who am I to…"

My aunt once told me that this question is a time-honored tradition of the women in our family. We doubt our qualifications for everything we want to do and our right to do it so we sabotage ourselves before others might take us down.

If this resonates with you, consider that we each have a seat at the table of life, by virtue of our having been born. Are you standing on the edges waiting for an invitation? Your birth certificate is your invitation. If you don't have time to sit because you are rushing around making sure everyone seated has what they need, sit down and discover that it's not all up to you to provide for everyone else. Have a seat and enjoy the conversation, the collaboration, and the co-creation of a vibrant healthy world.

Rewording can be rewarding

Sometimes we pose questions to ourselves that aren't intrinsically toxic but could be reworded to be more skillful. For example, one of my students asks herself, "What am I supposed to learn from this experience?" I suggested asking instead, "What *can* I learn from this experience?" Do you notice the difference in how you feel when you ask yourself those two questions? For me, the first with its 'supposed to' creates a feeling of external pressure, as if other people, the universe or God are requiring me to learn, and that I'm not measuring up if I don't figure this out. 'What can I learn…?' is a more engaged and joyful way to be in the world.

Cause for celebration

Having brought these kinds of questions to your attention, you may become more aware of them. They have probably been so much a part of your inner landscape that you never registered them before, never noticed how harsh and limiting they are. This recognition is cause for celebration; it's not the moment to be the enforcer and say, 'Don't ask that!'

Instead, if you find yourself asking toxic questions, make note, and give yourself the chance to explore more fully when you have a quiet moment, perhaps after your next meditation practice. Don't expect that they will disappear just because you want them to, but your growing awareness and compassion will disempower them. They will take up less space and become less toxic.

EXERCISE: What questions am I asking myself?
After meditation, notice the patterns of your natural thoughts.

If a question comes up, notice its nature. If it is an abusive question, ask yourself: Is this a question I inherited? A question a parent asked of themselves or of me? A question posed by childhood playmates, a teacher, the culture at large?

This is not to place blame, but to recognize that it is a pattern, that it has passed through many and is now passing through you. You can send loving-kindness to the 'source person,' remembering that they received it from somewhere else and may suffer from it still.

Toxic questions are likely to appear when we are in a stressful situation, or when we are struggling with a problem or with disappointments. In the following chapters, I offer more skillful questions to ask yourself in those situations.

Notes

What toxic questions are you asking yourself?

Empowering Question #1:
What is my intention here?

Whenever you are feeling stressed, try this: Pause, center in, notice the breath, and then ask yourself, 'What is my intention here?'

This is an honest question and deserves an honest answer. The answer might be something like "My intention here is to punish ___________ for what he/she did." An honest answer will probably not be rooted in wisdom. If it were, we wouldn't be in such turmoil. But instead of giving ourselves a hard time about it, we can, if we have time, use it as an opportunity to investigate. If there is no time, it's an opportunity to send loving-kindness to ourselves and the other person(s) before proceeding to reset our intention to something wiser. Something like: 'To be present in this moment with whatever is arising, just as it is.' Or: 'to be compassionate with myself and others.' You can adopt or adapt that wise intention or come up with one that suits you. Just remember that words matter, and unkind words have no place in wise intention.

When to ask, 'What is my intention here?'

- When you can't help but say or do something unskillful, or after you have said or done something unskillful. You may find your intention is retribution, revenge, or self-protection from a perceived enemy.
- When you feel exhausted from doing so much for others, you might discover that you have been hoping to get praise, affection, gratitude, or admiration.
- When you feel threatened by the idea that you might not be right, or when being seen as right is more important than actually finding the truth. Questioning your intention helps you discover how afraid you are of not being seen, appreciated, respected, or loved.

Seeing our intention laid bare may be unsettling and activate self-loathing. But if we can see why we have that intention, it can activate compassion. When we recognize how dependent we are on others to give us a sense of self-worth, we might also see how unreliable that approach is. 'If you want something done right, you have to do it yourself' rings true here. Resetting our intention to be compassionate with ourselves and others guides us to be skillful in our words and actions. Setting the intention to be present in this moment, just as it is, frees us to live fully, not wishing our lives away or putting ourselves in danger because we're not paying attention.

When we question our intention, we can save ourselves and others a lot of suffering. By cultivating wise intention, we feel more at ease in the world. When we see that we are operating from an unskillful intention, we can reset our intention to the deeper one we have given ourselves.

How can we reset our intention on the spot?

Say you are at a gathering, and someone you care about but have difficulty with starts up with a familiar pattern of words that put you on edge and activate unskillful intention. In that moment you can notice the sensations being activated in your body (pulsing, blood boiling, pressure, etc.) setting you up to erupt in your own seemingly inevitable pattern of reactive words and actions. Sound familiar?

You may notice, especially if you are giving yourself the gift of regular meditation, your ability to pause and reflect upon what you feel called to do has grown sufficient to meet this circumstance. It doesn't take you more than a second or two to recognize the unskillfulness here. In that pivotal moment (and every moment in our lives is a pivotal moment!) you have several options: You can take the bait and let the pattern play out as it always has, leaving you and the other person feeling badly. You can shut down the process altogether, telling yourself how you should behave. Or, and this is certainly the recommended choice, you can notice all that is arising. You can see the other person more clearly, see the pain and suffering that brings them to this pattern of unskillfulness. You can let that insight activate your natural compassion for that person and yourself, thus resetting your intention. Then do or say whatever arises from that wise intention. Your gentle shift of energy has the potential to break up the pattern and open a more honest and heartfelt connection. You don't need to mention your process. Just allow it to soften, release and awaken you to the wonder of that moment -- any moment we can suddenly recognize the great gift of being alive, even when dealing with someone we have tried to avoid.

The problem with 'should'

One of the words that comes up a lot when we explore intention is 'should' (ought, must, etc.). Watch for this word in your thoughts and speech. It indicates that your intention is coming from an external source. How we are in relationship to other people is only authentic and heartfelt when we are attuned to our own inner wisdom. If we are stuck in a storm of inner messages about how we should be, originally encoded by external sources (family, teachers, peers or the culture at large), then how can we relax and connect with others in a deep way?

By listening in we discover inner aspects that seem to have conflicting agendas, yet all are intent on saving us, however unskillfully. Behavioral psychologists call these aspects 'modules', and we all have them, so don't worry that you have multiple personalities. When we cultivate spaciousness through meditation, we see them more clearly and compassionately. We allow each of these aspects to feel heard and respected. We can feel gratitude for their loving intention but hold their fear-based demands up to closer scrutiny before we act upon them.

Accessing inner wisdom

With spacious awareness, we can access our own inner wisdom which has a distinctly different quality than those other voices. Unlike all other aspects, it is not rooted in fear. You can tell the difference because wisdom has no urgency, nor is it strident or bossy. Instead, it is consistently peaceful and kind, with no schedule or agenda. It never makes demands. It only offers wise counsel, and only when asked. You could go through your whole life without ever hearing it if you never take the time to pause, quiet the mind and listen in.

Align with your wise intentions

If you have set wise intentions, check to see if you are aligned with them. If you haven't yet set your wise intentions, asking yourself 'What is my intention here?' is still a useful way to explore how you got yourself into this difficult situation. What inner aspect's agenda were you following? And what is that aspect's intention?

Taking the time for skillful inquiry can lead to a whole wondrous series of self-discoveries.

Notes

What comes up for you about your intentions?

Empowering Question #2:
What am I afraid of?

If we found that our intention, as revealed in Question #1, was unwise and unskillful, then we can see how fear caused that intention, and, in turn, the resulting words or actions that created unhappiness all around.

Rooted in fear, we may feel tense, stressed, depressed or frantic. Or perhaps we procrastinate, not knowing why we can't bring ourselves to do something we want to do. Fear can cause us to become violent, even if the violence is veiled and turned in on ourselves. When we feel out-of-control, asking ourselves the question 'What am I afraid of?' is an effective way to see the fear that has been causing us to make poor choices and miss out on joy.

At first, our inner investigation will bring up stories about everything that the future could manifest, given current causes and conditions. None of us knows what the future holds, but we can see from our own experience how reacting fearfully sets up a pattern of fear, ill will and behavior we will later regret. Out of fear, we make enemies of everything. We spark fear in others, and they then react in ways that are unskillful, causing more fear in us, and more justification for our fear. Fear creates its own proof! But that doesn't mean it is the truth. It only means we are powerful and need to be aware of that.

Powerful? Yes! Beyond our wildest imagining. Often, especially for women, this power may be difficult to recognize. We have historically been marginalized, patronized, and disempowered. Those messages still run through us, no matter how liberated we may feel. Men can feel powerless too, and that powerlessness can turn destructive, angry, and irrational.

"Our deepest fear is not that we are inadequate. Our deepest fear is that we are powerful beyond measure. It is our light, not our darkness, that most frightens us. Your playing small does not serve the world. There is nothing enlightened about shrinking so that other people won't feel insecure around you. We are all meant to shine as children do. It's not just in some of us; it is in everyone. And as we let our own lights shine, we unconsciously give other people permission to do the same. As we are liberated from our own fear, our presence automatically liberates others."

— Marianne Williamson

True inner power is not dependent on external validation. Just by being alive, we are a powerful presence. Every being has the capacity to change the energy around them. Don't believe me? See if you can remember some gathering — family, business, friends — where everything was going swimmingly, or where everything was boring, until someone walked in and the energy was turned upside-down. The new addition, probably without even being aware of it, brought in fear-based antagonism or love-based *joie de vivre* that changed everything. It wasn't that the person was in a position of hierarchical power necessarily, but they, and we, are all powerful beyond measure. So, we need to take responsibility for the power we bring into the world.

If we are living in fear, we discount our power, and our actions (or lack of actions) may be misinterpreted. I was in a situation recently where I was impressed by the skillfulness of a young woman I sat next to when I took my granddaughter to gymnastics class. The woman had a toddler to keep quietly entertained and contained for an hour while her daughter attended the class, and she managed it so beautifully. Anyone would love to have a mother like that, and I wanted to tell her so. But I didn't. I fell back into a pattern of shyness, discounting my own power. I thought that my words would be awkward and unwelcome somehow. Later I regretted not saying something; we all appreciate praise, even if we don't seem to. The following week I was able to speak up and my compliment was well-received. Why did I initially withhold the compliment? Out of fear.

Another fear-based pattern is how we can misinterpret the impact we make as something external, something happening to us rather than something we are bringing into the situation. For example, the person who walks into a room of people, timid and shy, afraid of what people might think of them, may shrink and hide in such a way that people assume they want to be alone or consider the group unworthy of their time. So, they leave the person alone or may get defensive, depending on their own level of fear. This is interpreted by the 'interloper' as hostile, confirming their original feeling that they are not wanted there. What a difference a fearless person makes in such a situation, able to step up to welcome a person regardless of what they are projecting. But you can't always count on finding a fearless person; it's more skillful to simply be one!

This is a mild example. In the extreme, any person living through a filter of fear can activate fear in others, especially those who are already hyper-fearful. In some relationships, the two call out to one another, creating a dangerous bond: a shared scary world view that plays out a painful pattern of perpetrator and victim, again and again. This is not to blame the victim for what happens to them, but to acknowledge that fear attracts fear, and to encourage us to notice it. Question whether fear is performing a useful function, like looking both ways before we cross the street, or if it is activating patterns of harm. A fearful world view leaves people vulnerable to those who would seize power by activating that fear and using it to build up their own sense of fortified self. That never turns out well.

Looking at these patterns, we might wonder how we survive as a species with so much fear-based miscommunication. We survive with the power of love. This is not the acquisitive lust for stuff and domination, but the expansive love for all beings that rises out of gratitude for being alive in this moment, and the pleasure of sharing the joy with others who are alive with the sensate wonder of this amazing gift, just as it is.

Where does fear grab you?

- By the throat? Keeping you from speaking up?
- By the stomach? Keeping you from taking a chance on doing something you long to do in your life?
- By the heart? Keeping you from expressing your feelings, risking rejection?

These fears feel valid. They each have risks. But how much risk-aversion is smart, and how much is crushing you? That's an important exploration.

Through the practice of being fully present to notice thoughts and emotions as they arise and fall away in our experience, we can see fear for what it is. That awareness softens the tight grip that fear holds. What a relief!

Three ways fear causes suffering

The Buddha in his own inner investigation was able to identify what he called the 'three poisons' that cause suffering. As we look at each, we can see that they are all rooted in fear.

Desire, fear's greedy spawn

You may be surprised to see desire as rooted in fear. But think about the nature of desire: it is based in a sense of lack, of not-enough, and the assumption that something we acquire will remove that sense of lack. But desire is a mental pattern that breeds itself. My granddaughters will never have enough of the current collectible stuffed animals. Ever. They may think there is some amount that will satisfy, but that will happen only when the focus of their desires moves on to the next toy of the moment, and, way down the road, maybe the next crush, cute pair of shoes or who knows what of the moment. Oh my. It is so much easier to see desire's unwanted effects in children than it is to see them in our own lives. But desire is there, rooted in fear, causing suffering.

Aversion, fear's picky offspring

Fault-finding is a pattern that radiates out into the external world but is seated in our own sense of not being good enough. Those standards we set that the world is not measuring up to? They came from our own sense of not measuring up to our standards, set by some powerful person in our childhood, who was caught up in the pattern from their own childhood sense of failing, and on, and on. Getting caught up in blame is not useful. No parent or teacher has ever been perfectly skillful--well maybe that young mother at gymnastics class I mentioned earlier but I'm sure even she has her moments of unskillfulness at the end of a difficult day.

Delusion, fear's wayward child

If a person is zoned out or just seems blind to the world around them, it might be reasonable to assume there is something scary that they would rather not look at too deeply.

Since desire, aversion and delusion are the cause of suffering and are rooted in fear, the question 'What am I afraid of?' is a valuable exploration, but it might feel a little scary to pose. It may feel like having a conversation with the proverbial dragon at the gate, the one we've been avoiding or trying to sneak around for fear of getting scorched by its mouthful of flames. But if that resonates, then this is just the conversation we need to be having. Because beyond that gate is the interior life, we have been hiding from ourselves with our unquestioning patterns of fear.

Ask again

'What am I afraid of?' is not a one-off question. We can ask it, let the answer rise, and then, instead of getting overly caught up in analysis, justification, or argument, simply ask it again. And again. If you feel reluctant to go deeper in this way, remember that fear is already causing you pain. There's a gospel song, 'It is so high you can't get over it, so wide you can't get around it, so low you can't get under it. You've got to go in through the door.' The questions in this book are doors.

Disaster Preparedness

Letting fear dictate our lives isn't even helpful in addressing practical concerns like being prepared for emergencies. Instead it paralyzes us, making us unable to do what we need to do: create an emergency kit, build up a savings account, get a physical, make a will, etc.

What causes the paralysis? Under that fear is another fear. We may have the delusional idea that preparing for something will make it happen.

Through exploration, either on our own, with a friend, with a group, or with a therapist, we come to understand that we cause ourselves and others suffering through reacting out of fear. Gentle investigation may reveal that we are afraid of disappearing. So: we panic when someone disrespects us and when things around us change, causing us to cling to the world we know and push away new experience as threatening.

The Antidote to Fear

Just as fear is at the root of the three ways we suffer, the antidote to fear is offered in deep insight into the nature of things:

We are afraid of things changing or not changing. But nature teaches us that impermanence is the way of all things. The seasons change. All beings cycle through life, death, decay and the regeneration of new life in some other form, the way fallen trees fertilize the forest floor.

We are afraid of being isolated or separate. But nature teaches us that life is a complex web of patterns and networks that are not just interconnected but are inherently one system of being, active, alive and non-isolatable. We forget that our being is woven into the pattern of life. Each of us can be imagined as a fleeting shining shimmer of a jewel in a complex network, radiating and reflecting all life.

We are afraid of pain. How can we not be? It is a biological imperative to fear pain so that we avoid what could harm or kill us. But nature teaches us that the pain of being born into a body, of illness, of aging, and of dying are intrinsic parts of the great gift of being alive to experience all the ever-present richness of each moment of awareness.

Coping with pain

As we come more fully into the present moment, into the senses, we can begin to look more closely at the nature of pain. We let go of the very loaded word 'pain' and sit with the pure sensation. We start to notice that it is not just one sensation but multiple sensations, like instruments in an orchestra, each playing their parts. These smaller sensations are rarely in and of themselves painful. We find words to describe them more accurately: pressure, twinge, sharpness, ache, etc. We notice how they arise and fall away, and how another sensation takes its place. We see the nature of impermanence.

Our thoughts, rooted in fear, compound pain. On top of that pure sensation, we put the thought rooted in past experience: 'Oh no, not this again! I hate when this happens.' By then it's not just this sensation, but a whole series of past similar pains that we are dealing with all over again. Then we add in thoughts of the future: 'How long will this pain go on? Will I have to miss that event I want to go to? Is this going to be a thing recurring for the rest of my life? Kill me now!' And of course, we could toss a little comparing mind in there: 'Why am I the only one who suffers in this way? Why me?'

By bringing ourselves fully into the present moment, not making things worse by diving into past and future thoughts, we find a fresh, fearless way of being with pain. And then the pain disappears or turns into something else. Because life is impermanent, and pain too shall pass.

If a pain gets too difficult to focus on, we can notice what other sensations are present in other parts of the body – possibly pleasant or neutral sensations. This gives us a little relief, but also a reminder that there is more going on than just pain. We expand to include all of what is arising in our field of experience.

Gentle compassionate investigation after the regular practice of meditation is how we gain insight. And our insights, the ones that arise out of our own experience, are the ones that spark awakening, self-compassion and a sense of wonder that is fearless.

Befriend what arises, and be the light

When we're paying attention, it can be surprising how much fear in all its guises is present. We experience it as physical tension as if we are afraid the body will fall apart if we don't lend extra holding power. We experience numerous fear-based emotions: anger at another driver for putting us in jeopardy, anxiety over what people might think of us when we speak up, fear of being judged and found wanting, fear of getting ill, fear of dying, of losing a loved one, etc. etc.

The more aware we are of the fear the more we can be with it and acknowledge it. We're not pushing fear away. If we were afraid of snakes or rats, spending time in a controlled environment with an individual snake or rat, as uncomfortable as it might be at first, would help to soften the fear, wouldn't it? So much of our fear is rooted in our distrust of the unknown, so getting to know what we fear shifts us into a different frame of mind. We might still be cautious; we might never want to have a pet snake or rat. But something has shifted. That shift disempowers the fear.

Taking your seat at the table

While fear can activate us, motivating us to do something unskillful or half-hearted, it can also paralyze us and keep us from doing things in our lives. Fear has at times paralyzed me from living the full expression of this gift of life, from taking my seat at the table. This is the seat that is reserved for each of us just by being born into this world.

Male readers may not understand why this is even a thing. Boys are usually raised in such a way that they don't question that they have a seat at the table, a right to exist, a right to seek their own destiny. But girls historically have not. To the degree that is beginning to change, hallelujah!

One student who attended a women's march said that she had asked herself who she was doing this for. Another good question. She had felt since the Bay Area marches rarely got coverage beyond local media, why turn out? But once she was in the march, the most peaceful and joyful she had ever experienced, she understood that 'we were doing this for ourselves'. Now that's powerful! When we see the truth in that, we transition from trying to impress the powers that oppress us to *being* the power, to taking our seat at the table. She sent me some photos she had taken at the march and I enjoyed the many creative signs that the marchers carried. One that most closely aligned with my own message in my life and in my teachings said, "Don't curse the darkness, be the light!' In fact, amidst the little Buddha statues I've been given over the years, there is a small lighthouse to remind me of this meditative poem I wrote that is calming, centering and empowering. Try it!

Lighthouse
A Meditation

I radiate light
out into the fog
Air circles up and down
my staircase
Waves lap my shore,
storms pass through.
Just by shining
I am of service.
There's nothing
more I need to do.
I radiate light.

– Stephanie Noble

Notes

Can you be fearless in acknowledging fear?

Empowering Question #3:
Is what I'm telling myself true?

When we ask ourselves the first two questions -- 'What is my intention here?' and 'What am I afraid of?' -- the answers that come up shape the stories we rely on to navigate a complex inner and outer world.

Stories? Yes. Our minds weave stories out of what we experience with our senses. These stories are still full of the emotions we felt at the time they were formulated or first received. Scientists now say that the most distinctly human trait is the way we organize our experiences into stories that we then tell ourselves, each other, and our descendants. Over thousands of years, we have co-created a variety of cultures based on the collective stories that guide, enrich, enrage, and entertain us. These shared stories greatly influence us as we create our personal stories to interpret and understand what we are experiencing.

Clarification on the word 'story'

Calling our long-held patterns of thought 'stories' is not to discredit them or throw them out. It is to allow some light in so that we can see more clearly. If we've always accepted the story whole-cloth, how interesting to look more closely and see the distinct threads woven together to create the pattern.

When we ask, 'Is this true?' it is not to get rid of the story. It is to look with compassion and clarity at all the assumptions within the story. Most of our stories have both aspects of truth and aspects of misunderstanding or misinformation within them.

Teacher and author Byron Katie has made it her life's work helping readers and students question *Is it true? How do I know it's true?* and *Who would I be without my story?* That last question helps us to see how tightly we hold onto even the most painful stories. The story might be 'I'm a total klutz' or 'I'm the kind of person who could never do something I very much would like to.' These self-defining belief-stories are hard to challenge. We've built a lifetime

of 'proof' that backs up our story. This kind of inquiry can seem threatening: if I'm not this story I so passionately believe in, then who am I? And yet, some deeper wisdom within us encourages us to explore, to question, to open to the possibility that we are not a total klutz at all.
This inquiry is a gentle and incremental process, it isn't tearing up the book of our lives and writing a whole new version. It's an invitation to be present with what arises and a willingness to look with open eyes and open heart. We hold ourselves in kindness. *May I be well. May I be at ease. May I be at peace. May I be happy.*

Think of any strong experience you have had recently. You have most likely gone over it in your mind many times. Each time, maybe without realizing it, you refine and revise how you tell the story of that experience and how it fits in your life. This is the way the mind works: it processes experience. This may be a tale of some wonderful experience that you can recount at dinner parties, but more often the stories we weave are the ones based on challenging experiences, ones full of strong emotion. Why? Because they most need our attention to fully process.

I will use a personal example: I recently found myself rethinking the whole traumatic experience of the last week of my brother's life, when loving dedicated family and friends gathered in our home to give him hospice. At the time, I couldn't help noticing that while on the calendar it was a week, for me it felt like ten years. Intense emotional content paired with physical exhaustion can alter our experience of time, trying to make room for it all. This sense of time being elastic, of expanding when what we are going through becomes too much to immediately process, feels odd but is normal. It means we need to give ourselves time and compassion.

A few months after my brother died, I attended a writers' retreat. In that safe dedicated space, I was able to process more of my experience through writing poems. (Poetry has always been my most reliable means of inner exploration, but it's certainly not the only form to be useful in this way.) The retreat teacher, Kim Stafford, encouraged us to go deeper, to tell the hidden story. So often our instinct is to make our story 'nice' and inoffensive. We are in a rush to resolve our feelings, get past the discomfort and get on with our lives. It's as if we want to just put it all in a blender to make a smoothie so that it will be easier to swallow. But that doesn't work in the long run, does it? We need to take the time to digest experience. This is not to dwell on things or mull them over incessantly, but to give trauma — where there was so much to process in so little time — the chance to settle into not just a story we can live with, but into the most honest account as we understand it in this moment.

Which brings us to 'Is this true?' — a powerful question we can use in every situation. When we assess incoming information about the world around us, do we just accept what we read or hear? Are the filters we use to process the information prefabricated, so things we hear that resonate with our biases are accepted without question, and things that go against our biases are rejected without question? This is obviously an important use of the question.
But 'Is this true?' is also a way to look at what we are telling ourselves, at the stories we have stirred up with our questions 'What is my intention here?" and "What am I afraid of?"

At first, the inner story we uncover might be full of remorse, self-blame, or anger at someone else, imagining what we or they could have done differently. Or it might be full of self-righteousness and an unwillingness to look at more aspects of the events upon which the story was based. A gentle but firm 'Is this true?' can soften up the calcified shards of painful story we have been clinging to without realizing how much it has been coloring our perception of the world, perhaps blinding us to a simple truth that could help us see more clearly and compassionately. How does this happen?

The Faulty Filing System

Every day we file new information to make room for the next experience. For example, we pass a tree and, instead of really looking at it, we file it away under 'tree,' often so quickly we can't remember seeing a tree at all. If we are interested in trees, our filing will be a little more refined, noting its species, for example, and feeling a little pleasure in the knowing. But chances are we don't pause in our thinking mind and our busy day to ponder the tree, to question our assumptions about it unless it's a rare sighting of something we care about or have never seen before. We want to know what it is, because until we know what it is, we don't know where to file it. If it's like something else we know about, we classify it and attach it to our existing knowledge base. Then we have a growing system of preset stories -- based on culture, family, and personal experience -- that we rely on to guide us in all matters of internal filing.

Do you see any potential flaws in this system?

Here are a few that I can see:

1. If we are on autopilot as we process experience, the information is not properly vetted, is it? 'Garbage in, garbage out.' How could it be otherwise?
2. If the system is overloaded, it doesn't always file things correctly.
3. If the original formative stories were faulty and have never been questioned, then how can we expect this filing system to work at all?

To avoid 'garbage in, garbage out' we stay as present as we can with our senses in each moment, so our experience is processed without building up a backlog. We notice assumptions arising with the rest of what is going on, and we can question their veracity. This is not to undermine ourselves, but to cultivate spaciousness in our awareness so we can see clearly.

To assure things don't get so overwhelming that the system misfiles information and takes shortcuts, we take good care of ourselves. We get a good night's sleep, pace ourselves, meditate regularly, spend time in nature -- all with a receptive, responsive, compassionate sense of aliveness that helps us to make wise choices. When we can find balance in our lives so that we have sufficient alone time to process our experience, we stay 'caught up with the inner paperwork', so to speak. And we discover the joy possible in every moment.

Going through an emotionally stressful time puts this filing system to a real test. If we don't recognize that we need to give ourselves more time to process and catch up, the system overheats and short-circuits. If we are paying attention, we can sense when we need to pause, spend time alone, take a walk, journal, have a conversation with a trusted friend or seek the guidance of a counselor or therapist.

Now let's look at the third potential flaw in our filing system: How the original setup of our filing system may be flawed. Uh oh! That can't be good. But it's not life-threatening, we just have to be willing to look at what arises in a friendly way.

Think about those toxic questions we have been posing most of our lives. We don't have to struggle with them. We simply set the intention to stay present, noticing and then gently questioning the veracity of the stories we received and accepted as children, and the stories we have constructed over the years to attempt to make sense of the world.

As part of the care team for our youngest granddaughters since their births, I have had the joy of watching the way a child's brain processes information. Oh my, as bright as they are, how easily they can misunderstand things! For example, a few Decembers ago, when we picked up the four-year-old from her Lutheran preschool, I asked her what she was learning about Christmas. She said, "Well, Grandma, there was this lake of flames…"

Wha'? Okay, I'm sure that's not what they were telling her about the birth of Jesus. That misunderstanding, and the confidence in what we believe with all our heart to be true, is emblematic of the way our brains receive and process information as children. Then we get busy with our lives and never question our misinformed perceptions again. No wonder we get in trouble!

I hope this sharing helps you to be a bit suspicious of your stories that you understandably accept as not only true, but perhaps sacred in some way. Questioning them might feel like a threat to tear down your whole being. Think of it more like spring cleaning, lightening the load of the useless and often painful clutter of misinformation we all carry around. If you're not tossing it out, at least hold it more lightly and see it more clearly.

We all have a lot of stories. Our purpose is not to replace one story with another one. The question *Is this true?* allows us to soften the rigid stance that hasn't supported us very well. By exercising the mental muscles of compassionate and clear-sighted inquiry, we become more authentic and fluid. If we can allow for the possibility that a thought we've held for a long time is just an unexamined habit of mind, then we're not bogged down in defending the fortress we hold ourselves to be.

For a little inspiration, here is a classic tale that challenges our habit of reacting to life by fabricating stories about things that can't be known.

> A farmer's horse gets loose from the corral and disappears. The farmer's neighbor says, 'What a calamity! Poor you, stuck without a horse to plow your fields.' He is surprised when the farmer shrugs and says, 'Maybe yes, maybe no.'
> A few days later the horse returns with six wild horses in tow. Wow! Now the neighbor says, 'That's fantastic! What great luck!' The farmer again says 'Maybe yes, maybe no.'
> Then the farmer's son falls off one of the wild horses while trying to tame it and breaks his leg. 'How terrible!' the neighbor sympathizes. The farmer seems heartless in his unwillingness to

> claim this as a catastrophe. "Maybe yes, maybe no." The next week the army comes and takes all able-bodied young men, but not the son hobbling around on crutches. The neighbor cannot believe the farmer's good fortune.

We'll stop the story here, but you can see how it could go on and on in this way. The neighbor is weaving stories based on assumptions, while the farmer is allowing himself to be open to the possibility that the story is at the very least incomplete, even when it seems patently obvious to the neighbor what the truth of each situation is.

If you relate more to the neighbor, you are not alone. Most of us run with these stories, reacting to every change of fortune as a disaster or a stroke of luck. But there is a gift in allowing ourselves to pause in our automatic reactions to ask, 'Is this true?' and to see that the verdict is never in. We all have stories of misfortune that turned into great gifts. So, rushing to judgment is always premature. We don't know! And far from being scary or weak in some way, living in the 'I don't know' mind a most joyful state, opening a world of wonder.

When to use these questions

The three questions we have been looking at are helpful when we feel something's not quite right in our lives. For example, when we:

– have difficulty in a relationship
– get hurt feelings
– feel stuck or frustrated
– can't appreciate the goodness in life
– get caught up in thoughts of the past or future
– are hard on ourselves and/or our loved ones

Noticing when something's askew and asking *What is my intention here? What am I afraid of?* and *Is this true?* allows us to see more clearly what's going on. We may see where we are misunderstanding the true nature of our experience. This is not a fault-finding expedition, but a compassionate look with some clarifying tools we may not have realized we had on-hand to help.

Wise Effort

When we undertake this kind of inquiry, it's important to do so with wise effort. The answers won't be forthcoming if we mine them with a pickaxe. They arise in the space we create with our compassionate attention and gentle inquiry. This is only possible when we give ourselves time to quiet down, pause and unplug from our to-do list and our devices. A regular meditation practice can create the spaciousness needed, but the inquiry and the answers come afterwards, and at other times during the day if we are open and receptive to them.

This gentle patient inquiry is different than the 'Let's DO this thing!' attitude we may take when confronting a big project. There's no charge of adrenaline and no goal to aim for. There is no urgency in our inner investigation. If you sense an urgency, that's just a fear-based aspect wanting to get 'fixed' and be done. But this is not a one-off project. It's a rewarding healthy habit of a lifetime. Be compassionate toward that urgent aspect, but don't let it dictate the agenda here.

It's good to remember these empowering questions even if we feel present in our experience, not caught up in endless thoughts about the past or future. We can save them for the proverbial rainy day when they will come in handy. Most of us have at least occasional bouts of troubling emotions and circular thoughts, so these questions -- *What is my intention here? What am I afraid of? Is what I am telling myself true?* -- can be packed in the emergency kit for just such occasions.

Notes

Jot down any stories you tell yourself.
Notice the nature of your attachment to them,
why you feel you need them to be true. Then gently,
kindly, lovingly question whether they are really true.
See how it feels to soften your grip on them.

Empowering Question #4:
What am I cultivating here?

The first three questions in this series — *What is my intention here? What am I afraid of?* and *Is this true?* — are useful any time we feel we are on the verge of being unskillful in any way. Or we can use them if we feel we've been unskillful and want to see how that happened and how not to repeat it. These questions have to do with feeling safe within ourselves and in the world.

Once we feel reasonably safe, the next two questions help us find satisfaction in life. They are questions we can ask when we have time to be more reflective. They offer a way to look at how we are living: the 'lay of the land' of this inner and outer landscape we have created just by living.

We can look with appreciation at the beauty there, and with a gardener's discerning eye to what we might trim or plant to live with greater ease, harmony, and joy.

In every moment of our lives we are planting seeds and nurturing them. It pays to be mindful of what exactly we are cultivating, so we ask ourselves *What am I cultivating in my life?*

After meditating or a going for a quiet walk in nature, we can take a few moments for this inner inquiry. We can notice, for example, whether we are cultivating joy, delight, and gratitude. Or are we cultivating fear in all its variations and manifestations: greed, gossip, and hatred?

The word 'cultivate' accurately describes what we do in meditation. We cultivate spaciousness. We cultivate ease. We cultivate kindness and compassion. We don't push anything away.

When we are working in the garden, we discern between plants we have wisely planted and ones that popped up one spring morning and seemed pretty or benign, but in no time took over or spread everywhere. How often in life do we get into a seemingly benign activity that becomes a hard habit to break?

Consider where in your life some little pleasure has become burdensome, restricting and life-depleting rather than life-enhancing. It is skillful just to notice and consider the impact, as well as recognize other pleasures that might be more fulfilling. It is not skillful to beat ourselves up about not staying on top of these sneaky little weeds.

You reap what you sow

The word 'cultivate' is empowering. We take responsibility for the way things are in this moment and the way things will be in the future if these seeds come to fruition.

At the same time, just as a storm will come in and wreak havoc in a garden and then there's a period of recovery, we can see that it is not all up to us. Life is like this: impermanent by nature. When a life storm hits our inner landscape, can we accept the loss, assess the damage, and continue to garden? As we develop these skills, we may be able to even find pleasure in the small, sweet moments amidst the storm.

Neuroscientists recognize that we have a negativity bias that keeps us focused on dangers for our survival. But this life-preserving skill can also put us in danger if we forget to appreciate the joy and beauty around us, even in the most difficult moments of our lives. This is not to distract us, but to remind ourselves of all that is going on in this moment, not just the potential hazards.

Inner landscape design

While we have no control over when the sun will shine or the rain will fall, we do have the ability to adjust our plantings accordingly: ferns and azaleas in the shade, roses in the sunny places. We can assess the soil and information about the average rainfall. We can recognize that conditions change. A tree dies and is removed, and now this shaded area is sunny, so some adjustments need to be made.

When we come up against the loss of the ability to do something we love, can we find some other activity more suited to current conditions? Or do we get bogged down in a sense of helplessness and hopelessness, wishing things were the way they used to be?

Though there will inevitably be events and conditions beyond our control, by being present and noticing, we can make skillful adjustments to accommodate changing conditions, so that the seeds of our wise intentions have the best chance to grow.

It's a jungle in there!

Are you cultivating the seeds of your wisest intentions? Or are you just letting your inner garden become an impenetrable jungle? Beautiful in its way, but when difficulties arise, as they will in any life, it's daunting to try to navigate the tight twisted tangle of vines, the poison oak, and the possibility of slipping into a slimy swamp where who-knows-what is lurking. Oh my!! What foolhardy soul would go there? So, instead of spending time in the garden, we get up to all kinds of distracting, dulling and even dangerous activities to avoid the whole mess. Or conversely, we fall in love with the impenetrable nature of our inner jungle, fiercely clinging to that identity, as painful as it may be. We may think 'I'm mysterious' or 'I'm complicated' or 'I'm a mess!' Is this true?

The Pitfall of perfectionism

As you tour your inner garden, do you ignore the bowers of flowers and point out all the imperfections? It's a kind of blindness that makes us and everyone around us miserable. It helps to remember that the garden is a collaboration of the gardener and nature's own awesomeness. Green-thumbed gardeners are attuned to nature; they know they are nature, too.

A regular practice of meditation creates spaciousness in the inner garden, and through our practice, over time we are better able to cultivate compassion, balance, ease, and joy. We plant a seed in fertile soil enriched by our practice and trust that, with the regular watering of our daily practice and our intention to be mindful in daily life, the seed will grow. There is no immediate expectation: seeds take time to sprout. We're involved in the process, but we understand that it is not completely a product of our will. We are tapping into the nature of things. It is the nature of things to grow. It is within our nature to be peaceful, to have more clarity in our minds and more compassion in our hearts. We can see how perfectionism leads to paralysis.

Using the phrase 'cultivating spacious ease' can help to develop wise, balanced effort. If lost in judgmental thought, the phrase 'cultivating kindness' or 'cultivating compassion' can be helpful. Notice how different these phrases are from 'I should be kinder' or 'I should be more compassionate' or 'What a mean rotten person I am.' The word 'should' is a clue that we're looking through a faulty lens of fear at ourselves and the world.

Thinking of it as cultivation helps us accept that we are not necessarily always kind or compassionate in our lives, but we are cultivating those qualities. With wise intention, steady attention, and patience, they will grow within us.

Cultivation in all parts of our lives

As inner gardeners, we can use our question 'What am I cultivating here?' to look at all the areas of our lives. We might ask the following questions:

Am I cultivating health?

What am I cultivating here when I mindlessly eat more than the body needs in this moment? When I over-indulge in things that don't nourish? When I don't listen to the body's need to move, relax, sleep, wake, eat, have a symptom looked at, etc.?

What am I cultivating when I let a complex pattern of thoughts and emotions around self-image get in the way of attending the body's wise messages and caring for its simple needs? What am I cultivating when I obsess about any aspect of personal care?

Are there any aspects of my relationship to my body that are rooted in fear? Perhaps there is some genetic predisposition to an illness in the family, or perhaps you have had an illness that you are afraid will recur. Notice how much tension rises in the body from these fears. Will the tension itself cause harm? Relaxing and releasing may allow the body to heal and maintain itself optimally, and a mind that is not drenched in fear will be more willing to seek medical help as needed.

Am I cultivating healthy relationships?
In each family, friend, and workplace relationship, we can see patterns at play in the way we interact. We can see how we have cultivated warmth, caring and kindness. And perhaps where we have cultivated relationships that are thorny and difficult.

We may feel we are helpless to change a relationship, but it is worth experimenting to see. I know from my own experience and from students' reports that when we let down our defenses and instead send infinite loving-kindness in our thoughts to even the most difficult people in our lives, the energy shifts. This can be done from a distance. Any time that person comes to mind, just think 'May you be well.' This can be done not just with people we know personally but, for example, people in power with whom we disagree. This sending of loving-kindness doesn't condone their decisions. We can still write, phone and march to let our positions be clearly understood. But if our words are venomous and our actions are violent, then what are we really cultivating?

While we wish all beings well, some relationships are potentially toxic for us, and it's important to notice if, when hanging out with someone, we revert to unhealthy habits that don't support us — overindulging in food or drink, smoking or doing drugs, engaging in malicious gossip, spending beyond our means, etc.

There's no need to blame the friend. He or she is caught up in painful cycles and is deserving of our compassion. But we don't follow them into those cycles either. If we feel susceptible to temptation, we compassionately pull back from spending time with that person. Instead we send them infinite loving-kindness from a distance. *May you be well. May you be happy.*

We don't proselytize or try to fix anyone; we are each on our own journey here. But we can trust that, if we live true to our own wise intentions, we may, without realizing it, offer inspiration to others. And that is a greater kindness than giving ourselves away and losing ourselves in the process.

Am I cultivating a healthy work life?

The practice of meditation over time puts us in touch with our deepest, wisest self. Our fear-based efforts to be seen in a certain light fall away, and we grow into the fullness of simply being. The result is that we are authentic and accessible. Ambition to be seen as 'a success,' however we define it, falls away. Our work is a contribution to the world, a valued and necessary activity that stems from our abilities and interests.

Often in work situations, we might find we have patterns of over-exertion and exhaustion. Seeing what we are cultivating with unwise effort — the quality of the work product, the effect on our health, the effect on our relationships in and outside the workplace — helps us to develop more skillful balanced effort. Unwise effort is often based in fear, so revisit the question 'What am I afraid of?'

Am I cultivating a healthy community?
Taking responsibility for the wellbeing of our neighborhoods, cities, nations, etc. is part of being alive. Are we doing what is possible and necessary to do in this regard? Or are we thinking of the greater community as something apart from ourselves, something we prefer to complain about rather than take part in, even though it affects us greatly.

Am I cultivating a healthy planet?
Acknowledging our power includes taking responsibility for how our actions impact all life. If we belittle ourselves, we feel our actions don't matter, but they do. If we get caught up in guilt, we become paralyzed and unable to make simple choices to live lightly on the earth, making healthy choices, not poisoning the communal garden of our planet. So now that it is not only possible but easy, and even fun, to live more responsibly for the benefit of all life, why not do it?

Make room for wonder

These are just a few examples of areas you might explore with this question. See for yourself if asking 'What am I cultivating here?' gives you a valuable way of looking at your life. And whenever you can, practice cultivating spacious ease. Doing so makes room for wonder in our lives -- both the questioning kind of wonder and the awestruck kind of wonder. We make room for our own access to universal wisdom to whisper its truth to us in our most quiet, relaxed, and attentive moments.

Wise cultivation sometimes calls for transplanting

Among my family and friends, I have seen many examples of skillful cultivation. Some of them include transplanting. Just as an example, a man in his early fifties, whose professional life had been exemplary and satisfying, found his work situation untenable due to changes that were beyond his control when his company was purchased by an international conglomerate with different values. He worked hard to shield his employees from the harsher environment but found that the situation was taking a toll on his own health. He also recognized that, for most of his adult life, he had been living in the way he thought was expected of him. Now, with children raised and out of the house, he could assess what was working for him and what was not, and he found the strength to make needed changes.

Buddhist teachings encourage us to see that causes and conditions are not the source of our happiness or unhappiness. Believing otherwise entangles us in cycles of desire and aversion. Through our mindful compassionate practice, we befriend whatever arises in our experience.

But the teachings also encourage us to maintain healthy community and to steer clear of those who, for whatever reason, seem to thrive on toxicity. So, when we consistently greet our current situation with friendliness, when we do our best to collaboratively create a life-affirming communal experience, and yet at the end of each day we are miserable, the Buddhist answer is not to 'put up and shut up'. We are fortunate to live at a time and in a place where we have choice and the power to change our circumstances. That may or may not mean transplanting.

Recently my husband, the gardener in the family, noticed that the bougainvillea he planted last year was not looking healthy even though it was in a sunny spot with regular watering and feeding. With a little research he discovered that this plant wants to be completely dried out and then soaked, and it wants a different combination of nutrients. So, he made some adjustments, and a couple months later the plant is flourishing. It didn't need to be transplanted to have its needs met. But we have other examples in the garden where plants were just in the wrong place and, when moved, thrived.

Just so, a woman in her late thirties was so stressed out at work that she went to a nearby therapist, who assured her that she was not alone, and that he could write a book on all the patients he saw who worked for her company. This made it clear to her that no matter how much she tried to adapt to her circumstances, it would still be a constant uphill battle. Knowing her, I'm sure she did her best to brighten the lives of her coworkers, but she couldn't change the culture of the company. So, she found a position in a different company where conditions are more attuned to her nature, and where she feels valued.

It's important to note that in both these examples, neither person is in the habit of blaming external conditions for their own unhappiness. They are collaborative cultivators of creative solutions. Only after careful self-examination and a clear eye to all that was going on did they conclude that external change in the form of a transplant needed to happen.

How do you know when it's time to transplant?

When you're leaning so far over to get a little sunshine that you're practically flat on the ground. When new leaves wilt before they have a chance to open. When you feel choked, stressed from the heavy competition of more aggressive plants. Transplanting is not running away from life; it's getting a clearer view and making needed adjustments.

Of course, it would be great if transplanting weren't necessary. A well-planned garden considers the nature of the plants and all conditions. But life isn't always like that--okay, life is rarely like that. Maybe a little initial research would have revealed that one plant would eventually overshadow its neighbors, or that it has runners that make it invasive. In our lives we can choose our next move wisely, but there are often things that we couldn't have known. Instead of giving ourselves a hard time, complaining about the situation, or distracting ourselves with mindless entertainment and overindulgences to compensate ourselves for our misery; we assess, research, do some inner inquiry and see what needs to happen. Then we make it so.

Jon Kabat Zinn's book title 'Wherever you go, there you are' is a reminder that all the changes in the world will not correct a habitually unfriendly way of relating to the world. If we make a big life change, hoping it will solve all our problems, but then neglect to put in the time to cultivate spacious ease and compassion within ourselves and in all our relationships, the results will be a disappointing repeat performance of our previous experience.

In a slump? Quick ways to enliven your life

When we ask ourselves 'What am I cultivating here?' we might see that we are feeling down. Instead of succumbing or battling with the emotional cloud as we might be inclined to do, we can shift gears and do something different, something that uplifts or energizes us.

Choosing a skillful way to shift your energy is an individual choice, depending on what kinds of activities amp up joy for you. Here are some examples:

Meditation — even if you only have five minutes — will make a difference.

Music — listening to it, making it, dancing to it — is a powerful way to shift energy. Have your favorite music handy! I remember my mother used to put classical music on and do her version of ballet around the house! It worked wonders to lift her mood. I'm more inclined to rock out, but whatever works.

A walk —Try to choose someplace away from traffic or the lure of shopping. No time for a walk? Shift the way you are walking through the grocery store. Notice the sensation of walking, as if you are doing a walking meditation. Notice all the colors of the boxes on the shelves and the piles of fruits and vegetables. Perhaps see it all as a painting. Putting an imaginary frame around a moment or a sight reminds us to notice it. Then remove the frame and walk into it. Life!

A hike in nature, a run, a swim, a bike ride — all of these can be skillful as long as you stay present with the experience rather than ambitious about getting anywhere or accomplishing anything.

Laughter — is powerful in changing energy. It may not feel like something you can just do, but it's been found that even forced laughter will activate real laughter, and that laughing helps the immune system. If you have people around you, all the merrier.
Be sure the laughter is not at someone else's expense. That only activates fear, separation, and cruelty.

Meaningful conversation — stimulates the intellect, deepens empathy, and thus changes the energy. This one can be tricky because many of us engage in conversation that drains energy. What is the difference? Notice for yourself: are you and your companion complaining, gossiping? Or are you exploring, being playful, collaborating in creative problem solving?

Creative expression — Any of the arts can change the energy, but only if we stay in the process rather than focusing on the result, which only activates tension and fear of failure.

Volunteering — shifts the focus, brings balance and cultivates empathy and connection.

What are things you do in your life that switch things up when you're feeling in a slump? Remind yourself to do them!

The Seed Catalog

When we ask ourselves 'What am I cultivating here?' wouldn't it be nice to have a seed catalog for our inner garden? We could peruse through all the pretty plants and pick one we'd like to add. Well, hooray, there actually is one! In the following exercise, you can explore and learn about the ten beneficial qualities that are inherent in our being, but that possibly got stunted, went dormant or have just been underappreciated. All are available for us to actively cultivate in our lives.

EXERCISE: Cultivating Beneficial Qualities

Take at least a few minutes to quiet down and center in or do this exercise after your regular meditation practice.

Now, one by one, take your time looking over the list of beneficial qualities.

With each one, pause, sense in and see how it feels in your body. Does it bring pleasure? Then you probably have already cultivated this quality. Does it bring tension or anxiety? Make note of that. Discomfort may indicate a need for more attention in this area. You may feel you could do more in many areas but recognize that some may be enough for now. It doesn't mean you can't look more closely at it in the future: our garden is always in process.

Since it is most effective to cultivate one quality at a time, rate them so at the end of the exploration, you can see which one stood out as needing attention.

What qualities from the following list do you need to cultivate?

Generosity

This word may bring up examples of ways in which you have been generous with your time, your money, or other resources. If so, you can mark this one 'sufficient for now'. If it brings up feelings of tension, anxiety, or shame for a pattern of withholding even when you want to be generous, give it a 'star' as something that may need more attention and cultivation.

Recognizing our innate generosity, we can compassionately explore any fears that arise from past experiences of scarcity, of being taken advantage of, or of giving to exhaustion.

Ethical Conduct

This quality may bring up examples of times you have been fair, considerate, and how in general you operate from your inner moral compass. If so, you can mark this one 'sufficient for now'.

If it brings up feelings of anger, justification, annoyance or shame reflecting on examples of unethical behavior; or if your ethical behavior relies heavily on words like 'should' or on fear tactics to keep you in tow, mark this one with a star.

It is only when we contract in fear, believing ourselves to be isolated and separate, that we think up unethical solutions to the challenges we face. It is skillful to see how these unethical solutions ricochet in our lives, causing pain and confusion. This reminds us to choose the simpler, clearer, and more compassionate path of ethical conduct.

Letting Go

This quality may bring up memories of relative ease with releasing objects, transitioning out of even the most pleasant experiences, and holding all relationships in an 'open embrace', loving without smothering. If so, you can probably mark this one 'sufficient for now'.

If, on the other hand, you feel threatened by the idea of letting go, and recognize that you hold onto objects, roles, habits and relationships in a very tight way, then you will want to mark this with a star.

We are naturally fluid in our nature. But we can get rigid and clingy when we vest our identity in our attachment to people, roles, habits, and objects. Our clinging makes us rigid and even more fearful. Then, we believe that this fearfulness is who we are and that the only way to remedy it is to cling harder, making ourselves and others miserable. But it is not our true nature to cling. It is our true nature to dance the fluid dance of life.

Wisdom

If you feel you are open and receptive to life's 'teachable moments' that spark insights, if you see how they benefit your sense of wellbeing, and if you are comfortable with not knowing all the answers, but are happy to live with the questions themselves, then you can mark this one as 'sufficient for now'. This is not to claim to be wise. It only means that you are growing it in your inner garden. It is taking root.

If this all sounds like gobbledygook to you, you might want to mark it as something to cultivate!

Wisdom in this context is the deep understanding of the nature of impermanence, the sense of there being no separate self, and how we cause ourselves and others suffering through grasping, clinging, and pushing away. If you have been meditating awhile, you may have had insights that can fall in one or more of these three categories of 'Wise View'.

Energy | Strength

If this quality recalls how you meet challenges with a balanced physical and mental strength to handle whatever arises, then you can mark it 'sufficient for now'.

If you often feel lethargic and overwhelmed, or you often feel restless, driven, supercharged, and always need to be on the go, cultivating more balanced energy might be for you.

We come into the world attuned to the body's need to be active, to rest, to be nourished. This understanding cultivates our innate balanced energy and strength. When we lose that sense of attunement, then we forget that we are strong and have the energy to do whatever we need to do in life, if it is wise, ethical, loving and generous.

Patience

This quality may bring up examples of how you can easily wait without getting flustered or upset. If so, mark this one 'sufficient for now'.

If the very word 'patience' has you in an inner tantrum, and you can think of many ways you are thwarted in life by slow drivers, busy doctors, long lines at the grocery store, being put on hold on the phone, planes not taking off on time, people not understanding what you're talking about the first time you say it, people not getting to the point when they're talking, etc., well, this is the quality for you!

We get impatient when we are trying to escape from our current experience. We want to escape when we are not open to seeing life as it is. We become blind to beauty of every moment unfolding. We become more patient through being fully present, aware of all life's gifts, and through compassion.

Truthfulness

If you feel you are aware and ready to question 'Is this true?' you can mark this one 'sufficient for now'.
If, on the other hand, you find it difficult to be truthful with others or you are unwilling to question the truth of what you tell yourself, mark this quality in need of cultivation.

Truthfulness is not telling lies, of course, but it is also noticing and questioning the long-accepted stories we tell ourselves. We explored earlier the question 'Is this true?' and discovered that we often inadvertently lie to ourselves by accepting without question our long-held opinions, etc. We can also notice how easily we accept things that resonate with our opinions, and how often they are steeped in fear. We each need to be aware of scare tactics used to persuade us to buy, vote or think a certain way.

Resolve

If you can follow through on the intention(s) you set, then you have a strong sense of resolve. You can mark this 'sufficient for now'.

If you find it difficult to follow through on intentions, and you have checked in to make sure the intentions are wise, then Resolve might be a quality you want to cultivate.

Without the quality of resolve, intention and effort tend to fall apart. Resolve provides a clarity of purpose and the ability to stay focused on the task at hand, seeing how it fits into the bigger picture.

Loving-kindness

If you practice sending loving-kindness to yourself, others and ultimately all beings, and you feel the welling up of that infinite quality so that you radiate it, then you can mark this one 'sufficient for now'– though of course you continue to practice it.

If you are uncomfortable with the idea of giving yourself loving-kindness, or sending loving-kindness to even the most difficult people; or you are caught up in feeling there's only so much loving-kindness to go around and you're going to reserve it for those who are near and dear to you or those whom you deem deserving, then mark this as something you'll want to cultivate in your inner garden.

If we recognize the infinite nature of loving-kindness, we attune to it and allow it to flow through us. It is our true nature when we are not caught up in believing ourselves to be separate isolated objects in a finite situation.

Equanimity

If you can think of all kinds of ways that you are balanced and resilient in life, how causes and conditions rarely throw you (or at least not for long), and if you can be present in the moment for each experience that arises, then you can mark this one 'sufficient for now'.

If you struggle and feel overwhelmed by what feel like ever-changing demands of modern life, and many times you'd like to just be on a beach somewhere, then this might be a quality for you to cultivate.
Equanimity gives us the ability to go through life's ups and downs with the understanding that this too shall pass.
Our true nature is spacious and able to hold all of life in an open embrace. If we feel out of balance, coming home to our true nature allows us to rediscover that sense of being able to be in wholesome relationship with all that arises in our awareness.

If you did the exercise, look over your notations. Of the ones you've marked as needing cultivation, see if you can sense which one is in most need of attention right now. Which ones activated the most difficult sensations, thoughts and emotions?

You might find you have marked two or three. As you look at them you may see a relationship between them. You might also recognize that you mistook one for another. For example, the qualities of “resolve” and “energy” could easily cause some confusion. Look more closely. Is it really that you feel weak and lethargic? Or is it a lack of determination?

I hope you were able to take time to look at each of these and sense in to sensations, thoughts and emotions that came up around each. If not, try this exercise when you have more time. Exploring any one of these qualities could be a life’s practice. They work together to bring about awakening to our true Buddha nature.

Cultivating your chosen quality

One way to incorporate a quality into your life is to add it to your loving-kindness practice, if you have one. For example, you might say to yourself, ‘May I be well. May I be at ease. *May I cultivate my natural generosity.* May I be happy.’ See how I slipped the quality of Generosity in there? You can do this practice at any time during the day, and at the beginning or end of your meditation practice. Or send loving-kindness to yourself at the beginning, then radiate it out to all beings.

You can recall your chosen quality whenever you are struggling, upset or conflicted. Instead of trying to change anything, see if you can cultivate that quality to help you face the challenge. You might be surprised how well it applies and how it provides an effective solution. If it doesn't, then perhaps the quality you've chosen is not the one you most need to cultivate. Choose another! But I recommend you work with one quality at a time.

Let 'shoulds' and 'musts' rust in the tool shed

Please do not take this list of qualities, these wonderful seeds to plant in your garden, as a to-do list full of 'shoulds.' It would be easy to give yourself a hard time about not already having grown these qualities, but that would not grow them. It would only send you out of the garden altogether, saying 'I'm no good at this kind of stuff.' Instead, when you find yourself being unkind, look at which quality would most help you here. Then cultivate it.

Wise inquiry, the most useful tool

Once you have your quality, here are some more ways to explore. Keeping the quality in mind, ask yourself each of our first three powerful questions: *What is my intention here? What am I afraid of? Is this true?*

What is my intention here?

Regarding your chosen quality, sense in and ask yourself this question.

Since I have been working with the quality of generosity, I will use it as an example for this exploration. I propose that the intention of generosity is “to give wholeheartedly.” Okay, this sounds good, right? Half-hearted giving sounds lame. But does ‘wholehearted’ put out the expectation that I should give all of myself away?

When we come up with an ambiguous intention, it could reveal why this quality has not been fully cultivated. If I perceive generosity as a finite gift, that by giving I will be depleted -- and maybe I already feel depleted -- then there is a misunderstanding here. And fear. Clearly, I need to reword my intention. Maybe I can begin with what’s already there. I do have generous impulses, but sometimes fear undercuts my following through on those impulses. So, my revised intention might be “to act on my generous impulses.” For some, this might be a permission slip to empty their bank account, but for me it is gentle encouragement.

What is already there for you that will help you get in touch with the essence of your chosen quality?

What am I afraid of?

Staying with the example quality of generosity, the question 'What am I afraid of?' might bring up thoughts about potential outcomes. 'I am afraid of going broke.' We might explore if there was a time we were broke and have deep-seated fears of reliving that experience. We may know a generous person who lives 'closer to the edge' than we would be comfortable doing, and we are afraid for them.

Beyond how being generous might affect our bottom line, there is usually some other justification that has to do with those we might be generous to. We might believe they will 'just fritter it away' or that 'I worked hard for that money.' Harsh judgments about potential recipients can be very effective in deterring acts of generosity. I have observed in myself generous impulses that are quashed by such opinions and judgments. Without making an enemy of my thoughts or the potential recipient of my largesse, can I simply be aware and compassionate with all that arises so that, whatever my ultimate decision, it is not arising out of fear?

This question would work with any quality. Say, the quality of "Letting Go." There might be the initial impulse to declutter our home, but then some fear-based inner opinions arise to shut down the impulse. Even just noticing the impulse is a big step toward cultivating the quality.

We don't have to 'do' anything right away. Instead, very gently, kindly, and persistently, we sense into physical responses, emotional upwelling, images from the past and imagined futures, with all their accompanying stories.

Is this true?

As we explore the stories that come up when we think about our chosen quality, we can listen respectfully, and then ask, 'Is this true?' This is not to make the story a lie or to call ourselves liars. Instead, it is acknowledging that we are not our stories, that we will not fall apart if our stories don't hold up to closer scrutiny.

Regarding generosity: what story do I tell myself that justifies not being generous? These stories arise from fear and are worth examining.

None of our stories are writ in stone. They were all woven on the fly by us and others at vulnerable moments. At first, this realization can feel threatening. If we believe our identity is a compilation of our stories, of course we hold them tightly. But with the practice of meditation over time, we soften into a deeper understanding of our nature, and we no longer see these stories as a part of the fabric of our being. As we are freed from the weight of them, we may feel as if we are standing in sunlight for the first time. We discover that it was fear that wove the stories we've clung to all this time. We've taken them for granted, and now we see they do not serve us.

See if working with these three questions in a clear and compassionate way, helps you to see more clearly what has kept you from cultivating the quality you have chosen.

Cultivating with the core insights

In our garden analogy, we haven't yet looked at what is represented by the soil, the rain and the sunshine. This seems a big oversight! So, let's look at these most important aspects now:

The Buddha identified three characteristics of existence that, if understood, transform our whole way of being in the world. They are the underlying wisdom upon which all the rest of the teachings rely, and to which all the rest of the teachings point. On a graphic chart of the Buddha's teachings, these three 'marks', as they are also called, are at the very center. Every insight that arises, however simple or profound, will lead you to one or more of these three core understandings of the way of things.

What are these three characteristics of existence?

Impermanence

Things change and we don't like it. Things don't change enough, and we don't like it. Things change, we like it and assume now we will be happy forever, but we change in relationship to the thing that doesn't seem to be changing, and we're not happy. You get the picture. Impermanence is a fact of life, and how we are in relationship to it, to a great extent, determines our ability to be happy.

No Separate Self

Yes, you exist. But where are the boundaries of your being? The separate seeming nature of being is useful for practical purposes in this life, taking responsibility for this body, family, finances, commitments, etc. But taken to be complete reality, believing we are isolated individuals separate from the rest of being, causes suffering.

Suffering

While there is pain in this earthly life, most of our suffering we cause with our tendency to grasp at, cling to and push away all that arises in our field of experience.

(To read much more in-depth explorations of these three core concepts of Buddhism, called *anicca*, *anatta*, and *dukkha*, search my website, stephanienoble.com.)

For the purposes of our garden analogy, perhaps suffering is the soil. The quality of suffering is very earthy. We can get caught up in it, 'dirtied' by it and buried in it. Yet we can plant roots and draw nourishment from our deep understanding of the nature of suffering. Earthly life is not always an easy place, but as we put down roots, we become better able to sustain ourselves in it. We all experience suffering at times, through birth, illness, aging, and death. Think of something you have learned from going through something painful or difficult. Though we wouldn't wish it on anyone, there is something in the soil of suffering that causes us to grow. When we are experiencing pain in our lives, can we be fully present, rooted in the experience — not grasping, clinging, or pushing it away — but simply here to receive its nourishing message?

One time when I was in my thirties, my back went out. My pain was hobbling. Suddenly I understood that old people may walk slowly because they are in pain. Wow! For whatever reason, that had not crossed my mind before. My pain was a messenger. It cultivated an insight and compassion that has been of benefit to me in all my relationships.

For water, we could look to impermanence. Rain comes and goes. There are droughts and floods. There are clouds and clear skies. Water is constantly transforming: now it's ocean, now mist, fog, cloud; now rain, snow, sleet, or hail; now puddles, rivulets, streams, lakes, rivers, seas and back to the ocean. It's also present in all life, including our bodies. Accepting the nature of impermanence helps us to not make an enemy of all the inevitable changes we experience in our lives, our bodies, our relationships, and our world.

Sunlight could represent no separate self, that radiant light expanding infinitely in all directions.

What of air? Breath at the center of our practice is both a focus and a way to shift energy (releasing excess on the out-breath, bringing in enlivening energy on the in-breath). With breath we cultivate spaciousness, putting 'air' around our thoughts and emotions as they arise in our awareness so that they don't overwhelm us. Every plant in the garden needs sufficient air to thrive.

Through our meditation practice, the support of the teachings and our community of practitioners, we create the conditions for the qualities we have been exploring to grow and flourish.

Notes

Personal thoughts on what you are cultivating in your life.

Empowering Question #5:
What are my gifts?

Beyond the shared beneficial qualities we cultivate, we each have other gifts as well: the skills and interests that activate wholesome energy, aliveness, meaning and purpose. There is something inherent in each of us that draws us to different things. We can observe this in very small children; beyond the fun things most children enjoy, any individual child will be more excited about spending time in one or more activities and less interested in others: Drawing, writing, cooking, doing math, solving puzzles, singing, playing instruments, playing sports, listening to music, attending performances, taking things apart to see how they work, playacting, taking photos, doing science experiments, inventing things or walking in nature, for some examples.

But even though the adults around them may notice children's natural bents, gifts, and interests, often the children themselves do not see them, or do not understand that all kids aren't equally as interested in these things.

Some children zero in on interests, spending every spare minute on them. My husband drew and painted constantly from the age of three. But others are less clear. I was a shy little girl who enjoyed writing poems and short stories. I didn't play with dolls but loved making dollhouses and later drawing floor plans.

Bringing that little girl to mind now helps me to see where my natural interests are. I can think of what supplies, classes and guidance would be beneficial for her growth, and then provide them to myself now. I may come up against resistance – I'm too old, it's too expensive, etc. -- but to whatever degree I am able to live fully from my most authentic self, I deserve to try. And so do you.

EXERCISE: What are my gifts, skills, and interests
After meditation or after a few minutes of quieting the mind, ask yourself these questions and write down the answers that arise. Take your time. The first answer may

be the best answer, or it may be a toss-off answer and there's a deeper, shyer, truer answer waiting to be heard. All are fine.

Notice any resistance that comes up, either in the exercise or in anticipation of an exercise. You can use the first two empowering questions: *What is my intention here? What am I afraid of?* And, when stories arise about why you can't pursue a certain interest, look more closely at those stories, and ask the third: *Is this true?* It may seem true, and it may seem important to hold onto the story but look at every aspect with a kind but inquiring mind.

Okay, ready? Here we go:

1.Think of moments during your day, week, and life when you were filled with delight, contentment, purpose, enthusiasm — a sense of being in the right place or doing something satisfying. These will probably be very small-seeming things, but try not to judge them, just note them. List as many as come naturally to you.

2. Look over your list of moments of delight and think of them as belonging to someone else. Bring your most compassionate, least judgy self to this task. By observing the list as someone else's, we are generally clearer and kinder, more willing to see latent gifts we might deny in

ourselves. Then ask, what interests this person? What does this person love to do? If a clear picture comes to mind, write it down as a little summary.

3. Acknowledging that this is your list, not someone else's, notice any emotions arising as you read it. Notice any resistance to anything you have discovered. Notice any stories that come up to explain why, even if true, these interests and skills are for whatever reason, insufficient or not useful. *Several people in class felt they probably weren't doing this exercise 'right'. A couple thought their moments weren't sufficiently 'lofty'. This is not about being lofty! And it is not about defining yourself and presenting yourself to the world. It's more like the way a cat or dog might circle around to that just right spot of perfect contentment. Trust that whatever comes up is right for you in this moment.*

4. If you are judging yourself, finding fault or feeling resistance, ask 'What am I afraid of?' This is not a challenge, not a dare, but a compassionate investigation.

5. Send loving-kindness to any fearful aspect that speaks up or hides out within you. The inner critic may be powerful and cruel, but it is not your enemy. It is only afraid and unskillful in the ways it tries to protect you.

6. Looking at the summary you've made, do you feel that you are living your deepest most heartfelt interests?

7. If not, set the intention to give more time to them, incorporate them more fully into your life and whenever you are in such a moment, to not feel rushed but really allow yourself to experience it fully with deep appreciation.

8. Make note of any core interests you would like to explore more fully. This is not about 'becoming' someone new; this is not a makeover. It's recognizing what is already central to your way of being in this life, yet for whatever reason not actualized.

9. Set the intention to be compassionate with those aspects of self that are fearful, but don't let them run the show.

10. Save and revisit this list, try the exercise again another time, and consider rewriting it as a note to yourself to keep close as a reminder.

If you do this exploration multiple times, you may find different answers each time, but a pattern will arise that will hopefully inspire you to honor your natural gifts, interests and skills.

Notes

Jot down your answers to the exercise exploring your gifts here.

Take another look at the Marianne Williamson quote to see how it inspires you:

"Our deepest fear is not that we are inadequate. Our deepest fear is that we are powerful beyond measure. It is our light, not our darkness, that most frightens us. Your playing small does not serve the world. There is nothing enlightened about shrinking so that other people won't feel insecure around you. We are all meant to shine as children do. It's not just in some of us; it is in everyone. And as we let our own lights shine, we unconsciously give other people permission to do the same. As we are liberated from our own fear, our presence automatically liberates others."

— Marianne Williamson

Like many, I suffered from great doubts about my abilities. I kept my writing very private and never thought to share it with anyone. If I did share it, any compliments were like water off a duck's back: I have no memory of them. But even the slightest suggestion or critique cut me to the core and the scars were a constant reminder of my lack of talent. It's amazing I kept writing, but I wrote for myself to process my experience, and it was safe if I kept it private. And that's fine. Writing — and all the arts: music, visual arts, drama, crafts — all have the capacity to be cathartic.

We each have our way of processing the traumas of our lives; I imagine that working out mathematical equations might be cathartic, too. Can we find our way of skillfully processing and coping with all that arises in our lives? Hint: It will never be a distraction from what we are going through. It will not make an enemy of it that we push away. But it can be something that frees the mind from its ingrained patterns and lets possibilities float up to the surface.

Whatever kind of 'plant' we are, can we allow ourselves to bloom fully and radiantly? Can we notice when we get caught up in comparing mind, and relax and appreciate the fine qualities of other plants in the garden of life without wishing away our own?

Including all of who we are in everything we do

If we have a lot of different interests, it's easy to get stuck feeling we must choose just one. The expression 'jack of all trades, master of none' may come to mind. Feeling the burden of choosing can cause paralysis. It's more useful to see where the conjunctions are in our interests, where one might refine and support another. Can we broaden our perspective to see how these various interests and skills might form a more satisfying life? Some may not seem to go together, but a surprising number might. We just need to challenge some of our narrow assumptions. Perhaps some will play more supporting roles, but if they are life-affirming, they will enhance the ways we engage in life. Some that are somewhat hidden now may come to the forefront later. Who knows?

In that spirit, I have included an insight I had on meditation retreat that I wrote to myself as a poem.

No Thread Left Unwoven

On retreat at Spirit Rock

by Stephanie Noble

Dried hills weave
yellow ribbons
in the last light
They whisper
Leave no part of your being
unwoven in the fabric of your life

While the tidy seamstress with her
pursed lips full of straight pins
cuts frayed threads to the quick

The hills tell me
Even a weakness
can be a strength
How that hunger for approval
inspires me to offer praise

The hills say
Even a strength
can be a weakness
How that hunger for perfection
cuts away what is fine

Can I shed my shears?
Just let these threadbare tatters
weft at will through this life of mine?

The hills sing
Let it be so.

Post-exercise inquiry

If you did the previous exercise, look back over your list after a few days. Did any moments from the past jump out as reminders of something you could add to that list? Did any of the things you wrote down surprise you? Do any two or more of the skills or interest potentially combine in a satisfying way?

These are ongoing questions. If you didn't do the exercise, you might want to go back and give it a try. If you did it but it feels a little scary or troubling, then go back to the first three empowering questions and work with them around what comes up: 'What is my intention here?' 'What am I afraid of?' Whatever answers come up, look at them with fresh eyes and ask, 'Is this true?'

You might notice a harsh inner voice that devalues the gifts you name. There are often more than just one of these expressions of our fears, whose intentions are to keep us 'safe'. They can be thanked for their intentions, treated with respect and kindness, but not given the run of the place, because operating from fear is unskillful and potentially dangerous.

When we quiet down our busy lives and give our spacious attention to this moment, we may become aware of a quiet voice of infinite loving-kindness and wisdom. It has no sense of urgency. It never dictates. It simply offers guidance in the form of options.

When a harried inner voice sends us to the refrigerator for a little something, the wise inner voice might quietly ask us if it's possible we're not hungry at all, just bored? And if so, might we not consider another more uplifting activity.

But it takes practice to hear that quiet wisdom speaking amidst the cacophony of all those fear-based thought patterns going on in our brain. The more we listen, the more we recognize that wisdom, the more we operate from it, and though the other voices are present, we don't feel compelled to act on what they say (or at least not all the time!). As we anchor into awareness and compassion, we can even 'interview' them, discover their needs, and wisely negotiate some skillful solution that would satisfy them without sabotaging our wellbeing.

I remember my discovery of that wise inner voice in my meditation. Being fully present in the moment felt about as solid as dancing on the head of a pin. I fell off so many times, and the moments when I was there were so fleeting. But over time, with consistent practice, that pinhead grew larger and larger until I was able to be there most of the time, and I was aware if I was no longer there and knew how to get back in balance. The more I was able to be present, the more the inner wisdom grew and became primary, rather than hidden and heard only on rare occasions.

It may seem impossible at first: all those inner voices screaming and carrying on and laughing at the very idea that you could find wisdom within yourself. But the Buddha said "be a lamp unto yourself." He knew that each of us has the capacity to deepen in our experience, to cultivate presence, and to find that core of wisdom within.

Growing our capacity to pay attention

It is challenging. It reminds me of my aunt's experience with macular degeneration. She had adapted to seeing through just one eye, but suddenly that eye also went blind. Not surprisingly, she freaked out. But she attended a class and was encouraged to really look with careful attention. They told her to notice that there was a pinprick-size window of sight in the lower right side of her vision, and they trained her to see through that tiny window. Over time it felt to her as if the window must have grown larger, but it was only her capacity to focus there that had strengthened. That's the same with the practice of meditation: We grow in our capacity to pay attention, to be aware and to be compassionate with ourselves and others. And to recognize the access to infinite wisdom we each have within us.

Notes

Note and celebrate your gifts here. Don't be shy!

Empowering Question #6:
How can I help?

> *I have nothing to defend, nothing to fear, and nothing to prove. I have something to give.*
>
> -- An insight I had on retreat that has become a powerful reminder for me

Once we feel safe and satisfied, we can make wholesome connections. If we seek connection when we don't feel safe, we find protectors or victims.

If we seek connection to give meaning to our lives, then we find heroes, saints or gurus, and may develop an unhealthy, worshipful connection.

But when we feel safe and satisfied within ourselves, we are ready to connect in meaningful ways with others for the purpose of contributing from our bounty to the wellbeing of all. This is not a lofty goal. Think of someone you know whose little actions mean so much to you and others. No one needs to be a hero or a savior, but everyone can be a good friend, a dependable coworker, a fair employer, a contributing citizen, etc. There are all sorts of ways we reach out and connect to others. Here are some examples:

Finding friends

Making friends is easier when we know our own interests. We naturally find others who share those interests and enthusiasms. The internet and apps like Meetup and Nextdoor, not to mention all the dating apps, have made this much easier to do. But there are also local colleges, adult education programs, churches, and community centers. If this takes you out of your comfort zone, revisit the question 'What am I afraid of?'

Once we find a group we can meet with in person, we may develop friends within that group with whom the sense of connection goes beyond just a single shared interest.

Connecting with family

Deepening existing connections or reconnecting with family members who have been estranged can become a source of joy. Once we are not operating out of fear, deep friendships can develop between family members. It's worth questioning outdated assumptions and giving connection a try. Approaching an estranged or unpleasant family member can be scary but remember that they are operating out of fear as well. This will activate compassion, and that will shift the energy. Will you be new best friends? Who knows? But at least the relationship will be less toxic.

There may be a tendency to want to save a family member from their poor choices. This is a challenge, but it's important to recognize their autonomy and not insert yourself into their lives in a way that is not welcome. Again, just sending them loving-kindness, wishing them well, and not judging them, will go a long way to improve both your relationship and their feelings about themselves. You might think this is giving approval to destructive behavior but see if you can recognize how your wanting them to be different sets off their fears that activate negative behaviors. Of course, if they try to lure you into unhealthy or dangerous behavior, just send loving-kindness from a distance.

Being neighborly

Connecting with neighbors is not just convenient and enjoyable but creates greater safety. Don't wait for a crisis to get to know your neighbors. You may not share ideologies or interests, but you do have shared concerns about your immediate surroundings. Back in the day, neighbors knew each other because there was no television, no air conditioning and people typically sat out on the front stoop or porch, or hung out at the local park or pub, creating community. Now most of us retreat indoors, and while there are certainly pleasures there, a lot of sense of connection has been lost. The app Nextdoor has become a big boon to developing neighborly connection, but nothing beats getting together occasionally for a block party or other community gathering.

How can I help?

Connection is not about meeting our own personal needs, but about finding how the qualities and talents we have been cultivating can benefit family, friends, community, the earth and all beings.

Mr. Rogers is famous for saying that in a crisis "look for the helpers." The helpers are not just specially qualified people like police, firefighters, teachers, doctors, or nurses. Helpers are simply people who understand that we are all in this together, that we are all connected. They are people who feel safe, who feel reasonably satisfied with their lives, whose intentions are not grounded in fear. Helping is a natural extension of being alive in this world.

The playwright George Bernard Shaw, in talking about finding true joy in life, is quoted as saying "My life belongs to the community, and as long as I live, it is my privilege to do for it whatever I can."

A sense of connection is central to our deepest feeling of safety and understanding the nature of existence. If we cling to the idea of a separate self, we feel unsafe. We defend this separate-seeming fortress of self. If we do try to help someone else, it is from a finite depletable source, and our intention is to be seen as a good person, a nice person to gain approval, love, power and safety. But that's not the way it works, and we are left feeling more isolated and afraid. Instead, if everyone shared from that undepletable source, how joyously we all would live.

No boundaries

Where is the true edge of 'me'? The air we breathe in and out is shared by all beings alive today and throughout history. Skin is an incredibly porous surface constantly exchanging molecules with the rest of the world. Our bodies are intrinsic fleeting expressions of ever-changing electrical impulses and chemicals combining and recombining; complex systems, networks and processes generating and regenerating — birth, growth, death, decay, and new life, arising and falling away.

Our differences are relatively recent man-made distinctions for purposes of learning and examining, grouping shared characteristics into categories and divisions like phylum, class, family, genus, and species. This is a convenience for study but an inconvenience for in-depth perception of being. The same science that made those distinctions is now finding more and more connections. Just the other day I read that they have found that trees have heartbeats. Can we allow for the possibility that just because we don't have the biological or technical means to see something right now doesn't mean it doesn't exist?

The more we can sense that simple but powerful truth of our intrinsic oneness of being, the more we can rest in the gift of being alive in this moment, just as it is.

Loving-kindness

Sending infinite loving-kindness is one way we can help, even from a distance. It is a practice that always begin with us because we can't share what we don't have. If we try to give it away before fully receiving it, we are not giving infinite lovingkindness but some finite fragile wish that leaves us depleted. We open to the possibility of infinite loving-kindness readily available to fill us to full and overflowing. We say 'May I be well. May I be at ease. May I be peaceful. May I be happy.' -- or other blessings of that general nature.

Once we feel the infinite quality of loving-kindness filling us, we naturally share it. This sharing is a welling up and becoming a conduit for lovingkindness. It grows stronger within us as we share it. We think of someone who is need of extra loving-kindness, and we say, 'May you be well.'

Because this loving-kindness is infinite in nature, it can't be contained. It grows beyond our little circle of loved ones, out into the community, out into the world. It shines its radiant loving light into even the darkest places. It encircles the whole planet and beyond. And we say, 'May all beings be well.' Without exception.

With meditation, we grow in our ability to be present and compassionate. We don't feel separate, so we have nothing to defend, nothing to fear, nothing to prove. But we do have something to give.

When we sense our intrinsic connection to all life, fear dissolves. Whether we come to our understanding through studying science or we feel it intuitively, it's an understanding that makes a huge difference in our lives and in the lives of those around us.

See for yourself! Notice how someone's authentic smile or words of kindness affect your whole day. Notice how critical, angry fear-based words or harsh expressions affect you.

Can you recognize that *your* looks, words, and actions are equally powerful? Without realizing it, you are impacting all lives around you because you are intrinsically connected. Just by living we make a difference. The question is: what kind of difference are we making?

Coming full circle

In moments of danger, our deep understanding of inherent oneness brings out our instinct to help. In crisis situations, people surprise themselves with their unsuspected strength or the stamina to do what needs to be done to help.

We may like the person we become in a moment of crisis, whether it's the adrenaline rush that breaks us out of our rut, or the good feeling of being needed. But we don't need crises to be helpers. There is always someone in need. We may habitually turn a blind eye to the need. We may see someone in need but find fear activated more readily than compassion. Or we might not see the need in some people because they maintain a polished front. We may compare our messy insides with others' polished outsides, and we can't imagine they have any problems or that we have something of value to offer them. But we are all the same stardust after all. If we can reveal a little of our own feelings of vulnerability, then we find deeper connection and understanding.

We also can expand our idea of what helping is. In a crisis it is so clear, but once the crisis has passed, what do we have to offer? What about entertainment, inspiration, education, beauty, humor? If you have eased someone's mind for a time by sharing an enjoyable, funny, or uplifting experience in any way, that's helping! If others have benefited from your skillful sharing of knowledge and experience, that's helping! If you are part of a support team for the care of family members or friends, that's helping! If you clean up litter, if you make wise environmental choices, if you turn the lights off when you leave a room, that's helping! If you donate to caring causes, that's helping! If you vote, that's helping! If you take good care of your body so that you will stay healthy, that's helping!

Chances are you are probably already helping; you just might not see it that way. So much depends on your intention, which brings us back to the first question in this series: 'What is my intention here?' Whatever way you make a living, spend your time and engage with the world, when you question your intention, you may discover that you are indeed a helper.

Notes

How I can engage for the benefit of all beings in a way that is the best use of my gifts and interests?

Come to the end? Begin again!

I hope you have found these six questions helpful in gaining insight into your own relationship with experience, where any reactivity comes from and how to develop a greater sense of safety, satisfaction and connection.

I recommend that you revisit the questions often. Use the first three -- *What is my intention here? What am I afraid of?* And *Is what I am telling myself true?* -- as your go-to tools any time you feel troubled or feel you might be about to do something unskillful. The rest are for you to ponder as they feel meaningful. *What am I cultivating here?* is great for when you feel stuck, bored or disgruntled. *What are my gifts?* is a question to sit with for a while, after you found safety within yourself. And *How can I help?* is a wonderful way to greet the world, once you feel safe and clear on what gifts you have to offer. Of course, you may develop more skills and discover other talents as you offer help in the world, guided by your own wise intention.

I wish you well in your exploration and your life. Please feel free to contact me through my website stephanienoble.com with comments and your own questions about these six empowering questions. I look forward to hearing from you!

And please, if you found this book useful, review it on Amazon and Goodreads, share it on social media and recommend it to your friends. Suggest it for your book group. It is a perfect book to explore together, supporting each other in self-discovery. This is not something to keep to ourselves. The more people in touch with their own inner wisdom, the better it is for all of us.

May you be well.
May you know the joy of being fully present in this moment just as it is.

Always we hope
someone else has the answer,
some other place will be better,
some other time
it will turn out.

This is it.
No one else has the answer,
no other place will be better,
and it has already turned out.

At the center of your being,
you have the answer:
you know who you are and
you know what you want.
There is no need to run outside
for better seeing,
nor to peer from a window.

Rather abide at the center of your being:
for the more you leave it,
the less you learn.
Search your heart and see
the way to do is to be.

— *Lao Tzu*

A note about meditation

Throughout these chapters, I encourage you to meditate as part of the process of inner discovery. If that causes you to feel some resistance, you are not alone. But I hope that you will challenge your misconceptions about meditation and about your own ability to do it. It is a natural activity that is important for our wellbeing.

Thinking about starting a meditation practice may feel like another chore to do, like taking out the garbage or cleaning the kitchen. Both do require wise intention and skillful effort, and afterward there's a noticeable positive difference in our lives.

But they are also quite different, probably in many ways, but here's at least one: Chores are things that someone else could do for us if we didn't want to do them and money was no object. But no one can meditate for us. Just as no one can attend a concert for us or eat a meal for us. No one can enjoy a good book for us or go on a life-transforming trip for us. These kinds of things no one could do for us because they are not chores, but experiences that directly provide us with pleasure, nourishment, insight, and edification.

Meditation is a pleasure! This might not be immediately apparent because like many pleasures, we develop our deep appreciation of it through practice and exposure. Though some people find meditating easy from the start, for most it is an appreciation that develops over time. It is like acquiring a taste for walking in the woods if we've never done it and have only watched scary movies and the woods is where the bodies get buried. We may be afraid of what's behind a tree or around the next curve on the trail. Just so, someone who has never meditated may fear what might be lurking within their minds. But, as with the new hiker in the woods, practice increases awareness and understanding.

The new meditator discovers that being present with the senses in silence is a safe place to be. They increasingly find comfort in their growing ability to stay present with all the physical sensations, emotions and thoughts that naturally arise in their field of awareness. They develop the skills to greet all that arises with friendliness, to trust their own inner wisdom to help them see more clearly and experience more expansively being fully alive in each moment.

When it comes to chores, a regular meditation practice helps us to discover that even these tasks can be pleasurable. The pleasure isn't just the satisfaction of a job well done, but in the doing itself, living life just as it is in this moment with appreciation.

If you have no experience with meditation, or have had a negative experience with it, here is a set of simple brief instructions for mindfulness meditation.

Meditation Instruction

We begin by closing our eyes (you can leave them open with a downward gaze) and setting our intention to be present with our experience, and to be compassionate with ourselves when we get lost in thought. That's the basic instruction. It's simply sitting and being aware that you are sitting, continually bringing the wandering mind back to the present experience.

Anchoring awareness again and again into physical sensation is the essence of staying present. Notice when tension arises; breathe into it to gently release it to whatever degree is possible. When the mind wanders, *gently and kindly* reset the intention to be present and bring your attention into sensation. The breath is the most dependable sensation to follow. This is the valuable practice of embodiment.

In meditation you might experience frustration or boredom. You might notice expectations not being met. You might notice fear of not 'doing it right.' You might notice judgment of the experience. You might notice comparing this experience to another you've had or to something someone else said they had.

This is all fine. Just stay with noticing. It's not the experience itself but the development of our ability to stay present with it that is important. And like any activity, it takes practice, developing new 'muscles' we haven't really used before. Be as kind as you can be to yourself.

For more guidance, check out the meditation section of my website or download the Insight Timer app and follow audio instructions from me, or from any one of thousands of teachers.

Acknowledgements

Thank you to my meditation students and dharma blog followers who have been and continue to be on a journey of self-discovery with me. Because of you, I stay true to my own meditation practice!

Thank you to Rick Hanson, PhD, who after reading the manuscript invited me to teach it to his meditation group; and Adrian Emery who brought the physical book to life.

Thank you always to my family near and far, as well as old friends I consider family, all dear to me beyond measure.

About the Author

Stephanie Noble has taught Buddhist Insight meditation since 2007 and is the founder of Marin Insight Women's Sangha. She sits on the board of the Buddhist Insight Network. She has practiced, studied, volunteered, taught, and sat retreats at Spirit Rock Meditation Center since 1994.

The author of *Tapping the Wisdom Within, A Guide to Joyous Living*, she has been twice nominated for the Pushcart Prize in poetry. Her essays and poems have been published *Wise Brain Bulletin, The Buddhist Poetry Review, Light of Consciousness Magazine, The Mindful Word* and many other journals and anthologies.

Her weekly dharma posts can be read at Stephanienoble.com. Her recorded meditations are featured on Insight Timer.

Made in the USA
Las Vegas, NV
04 December 2020

12024452R00075